PICKERING
and
THORNTON LE DALE

A Practical guide for visitors
by
Malcolm Boyes & Hazel Chester

The Dalesman Publishing Company Ltd.
Clapham, Lancaster, LA2 8EB

First published 1977
Third edition 1991
© Text, Malcolm Boyes & Hazel Chester 1977, 1991
© Illustrations, J. J. Thomlinson, 1977

ISBN: 1 85568 029 7

Printed by Peter Fretwell & Sons Ltd., Keighley, West Yorkshire BD21 0PZ.

Contents

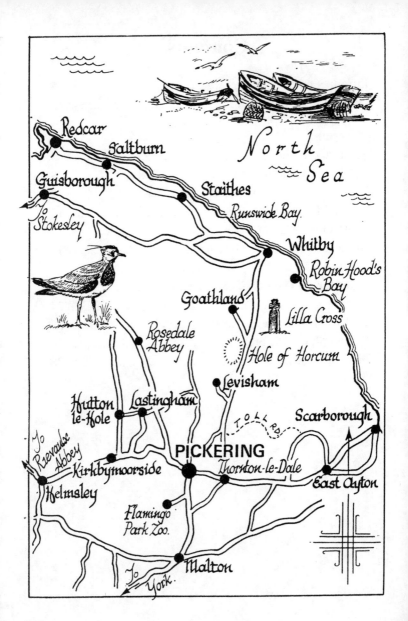

Redcar
Saltburn
Guisborough
To Stokesley
Staithes
Runswick Bay.
North Sea
Whitby
Robin Hood's Bay
Goathland
Lilla Cross
Rosedale Abbey
Hole of Horcum
Levisham
Hutton le-Hole
Lastingham
Scarborough
To Rievaulx Abbey
Kirkbymoorside
TOLL RD.
PICKERING
Thornton-le-Dale
East Ayton
Helmsley
Flamingo Park Zoo.
To York.
Malton

INTRODUCTION

Pickering and Thornton le Dale stand only two miles apart on the southern edge of the North York Moors National Park. They are excellent bases for exploring Ryedale, the Yorkshire Coast and the North York Moors.

Pickering is the southern terminus of the privately owned North Yorkshire Moors Railway which operates steam and diesel engines through rugged Newtondale to Grosmont. The interesting church contains some fine murals. There is a royal castle and a fascinating folk museum.

Thornton le Dale is among Yorkshire's prettiest villages. From the bridge over Thornton Beck there is a magnificent view of a thatched cottage which has appeared on many calendars. The Square has an old market cross and a pair of stocks, while the church to the east overlooks the scene. There are pleasant walks around the village and beside the stream.

Not far away is the picturesque hamlet of Ellerburn with its interesting church and further north is the Dalby Forest Drive threading its way through the North Riding Forest Park. There is an interpretive centre at Low Dalby and a short walk from Staindale Lake leads to The Bridestones.

GENERAL INFORMATION

Tourist Information Centre: Eastgate car park, Pickering.

Market Day: Pickering, Monday.

Early closing day: Wednesday.

Bus Station: Eastgate, Pickering.

Bus Services: Scarborough and District Motor Services. Services to Thornton le Dale and Scarborough; Whitby, Flamingoland and Malton; Helmsley and Ampleforth; and a local town service.

Rail Services: North Yorkshire Moors Railway operates a steam and diesel service to Goathland and Grosmont. There is a connecting bus service to Whitby. The nearest British Rail station is Malton.

Post Offices: Market Place, Pickering. Maltongate, Thornton le Dale.

Public Library: The Ropery, Pickering.

Car parks: Pickering – Eastgate, The Ropery, Vivis Lane and at the railway station. Thornton le Dale – Off Maltongate.

Toilets: Pickering – Eastgate, The Ropery. Thornton le Dale – Whitbygate. Low Dalby and The Bridestones car park.

Police Station: Malton Road, Pickering, or Malton 692424.

Fire Station: Malton Road, Pickering.

Golf: 9-hole course at Black Bull, Malton Road, Pickering. Driving range, Snainton.

Fishing: Licences and details from the Tourist Information Centre.

Cinema: Burgate, Pickering.

Theme Park: Flamingoland, Kirby Misperton.

Animal Park: Newton on Rawcliffe.

Riding School: Beck Isle Ponies, Pickering (winter only). The Hall Stables, Thornton le Dale.

Caravan sites: Upper Carr caravan site, Malton Road,

Pickering. Overbrook caravan site, Thornton le Dale. Old Ellers, Ellerburn.

Swimming Pool: Mill Lane, Pickering.

Children's Playground: Roxby Road, Thornton le Dale.

John Castillo's gravestone
(see page 15)

PICKERING

The Market Place

In the centre of the town and rising from Pickering Beck towards the church is the Market Place. The market takes place each Monday with stalls selling a wide range of goods. It is the gathering place not only for the residents of Pickering but for the farmers and villagers from a wide area.

As with many towns and cities the interesting old buildings have been adapted to more commercial pursuits. The stone built St. George's House used to be the George Inn. The passage down the side of the building which leads to Hungate is called Pirate Alley. The Conservative Club was built in 1830 by Nicholas Piper who made his money from whaling. In 1775 he, along with some friends, bought the whaling ship Henrietta. It sailed on a number of successful voyages out of Whitby. Some of the crew were from the Pickering area. In Champley Mews there is a number of small interesting shops standing on the site of the Albert Foundry. It was run by John Weighill who made ploughs, grass mowers, grinding mills for corn and other machinery. It was restarted in 1879 by Francis Dobson and continued making plough shares, kitchen ranges and frying pans until 1960.

There used to be a tallow chandler's works in the Market Place and when it closed the tools and equipment were moved to the Castle Museum at York. The White Swan is an old coaching inn. It was used by the *England Rejoice* coach before it crossed the inhospitable moors to Whitby. The timbered Bay Horse Hotel was a posting house where some of Cromwell's officers stayed during the Civil War. The old stocks used to be at the top of the Market Place, but those who brewed bad ale were placed in the ducking stool and lowered into Pickering Beck.

The Parish Church

Overlooking the Market Place is the tower and spire of the parish church of St. Peter and St. Paul which is surrounded by shops and houses backing on to the small churchyard.

Pickering Church from the Market Place

There has probably been a church on the site since Saxon times. In the north-east corner of the nave, near the lectern, is the recumbent figure of a knight in armour dating from the 14th century. This is William Bruce who founded a chantry here in 1337; his coat of arms can be seen on his shield. There are also recumbent effigies of Sir David and Margery Roucliffe in the Roucliffe chapel on the right of the chapel.

At the west end of the church, on the left as you enter, are two maps of Washington D.C. and a photograph of Robert King who was born in Pickering in 1740 and was baptised and married in the church. Robert King was the surveyor who planned the new city on a site chosen by George Washington. He was buried in Pickering on 6th December, 1817.

On the north side of the chancel are several brass plaques with American connections; two have been presented by U.S. Ambassadors to Britain. The town is on an American Heritage Trail specially arranged so that visitors from the U.S.A. can see places with American connections.

Immediately you enter the church you see the magnificent frescoes which adorn both sides of the nave and date from the early 15th century. For many years they were hidden under numerous coats of whitewash but were rediscovered in 1853. Over a number of years, from 1878, the frescoes were restored to their former glory. They depict various biblical scenes, the martyrdom of St. Edmund who was killed by 14 arrows and St. George slaying the dragon.

Burgate and the Castle

One of the customs carried out up to 100 years ago was "Riding t'fair". On market mornings the steward of the Duchy of Lancaster rode on horseback down from the castle to the market carrying a sword in a fine gilt scabbard; he was accompanied by two freeholders of the Duchy of Lancaster lands. At the top of the Market Place he would read a proclamation declaring the market open and that a Court of Pye Powder was in session to give judgement in cases of dispute. The proclamation was then read in other parts of the town.

At the top of Burgate is a small crossroads. You can turn right then right again down Willowgate back into the Market Place. John Wesley first preached to the inhabitants of Pickering in this street. To the left of the crossroads is Brant Hill, which descends to the railway station and Pickering Beck. The lane was used to bring water into the town. Burgate contains the local cinema which also operates a cafe.

The road carries straight on along Castlegate. On your left is a Quaker burial ground with a mounting block in front of the house. In the garden behind is the Friends' Meeting House.

Pickering Castle

The first castle was built on this site late in the 11th century. King Henry I visited the castle in 1106 and founded the Honour and Forest of Pickering, a vast hunting domain which extended from near the coast to Rosedale and from the river Derwent to the river Esk. In 1267 the castle, manor and forest were given to the Earl of Lancaster, who obtained for the town a fair that was held in Castlegate and the castle grounds. The castle declined in the 15th century; it declined further when Sir Richard Chomley removed 14 wagon loads of stone to build Roxby Castle near Thornton le Dale. Cromwell's forces took the castle during the Civil War but it was returned to the Duchy of Lancaster on the restoration of the monarchy.

The castle is now administered by English Heritage. On special weekends in the year there may be displays of falconry or medieval combats being staged.

You enter the castle across a dry moat and pass through a gateway into the Outer Ward. On the left across the neatly trimmed lawns is Mill Tower – the basement was a prison and the upper floor may have housed the jailer. If you turn to the right as you enter you can see Diate Hill Tower and further along the wall is Rosamund Tower. From the Outer

Ward you can walk along a narrow passageway in the tower and look down on the postern gate. A set of steps descend into the moat, which you can walk along to the postern gate entrance. A series of steps at the other side of the moat lead to the Inner Ward, on the right of which are the Constable's Lodgings. The foundations nearest to you are storehouses and near the curtain wall is the hall. Continuing across the grass you arrive at the stone-roofed chapel which contains a small display. Behind are the foundations of the New Hall rebuilt in 1314 for Countess Alice, the Earl of Lancaster's wife; it was a two-storied building with a stone roof.

Cross the Inner Ward to the railed steps which lead to the keep on top of the motte. Straight in front of you as you ascend the steps Coleman Tower, at one time known as the King's Prison. On the right going up the steps, you can see the circular ovens; on the left is the well set in the moat. The steps turn left and climb up to the keep. The motte gives fine views over the countryside.

Undercliffe and the Railway

As you leave the castle you have a view on your right of Pickering Beck and Beacon Hill, which was possibly the site of an earlier castle. For many years it has been used by the inhabitants of Pickering to celebrate victories and coronations. Among the many bonfires to have been lit on Beacon Hill are those celebrating the Battle of Waterloo, Queen Victoria's Diamond Jubilee, the Relief of Mafeking and most recently the Queen's Silver Jubilee. If you turn right after leaving the castle the road goes steeply downhill to the Undercliffe. After fifty yards, at the bend, you can turn left along a path which gives pleasant views towards Pickering Beck and the North Yorkshire Moors Railway line. On your right is a former watermill that received its power from an undershot wheel on a mill race off Pickering Beck. The wheel turned two pairs of stones to grind the corn. The two top stones each weighed a ton.

A little further down the road to Newbridge is the **Moorland Fun Fishing and Trout Farm**. You can spend a day fishing, hiring a fly rod and bait from the farm. You are able to feed fish or just watch them. Also you can take some home for tea.

Opposite the railway station is the Station Hotel. The building may date from before 1777 and was probably a beer house up to 1836 serving the workmen who built the Pickering to Whitby railway. Two railway lines support the upper floor of the inn.

A little further down Park Street is a **Model Railway Exhibition**. The tracks are set out in appropriate landscaped surroundings. Visitors to the exhibition can operate various trains and one display includes Thomas the tank engine. There is an Aurora AFX track where visitors can race the model cars and a display of Yesteryear model cars. This place will entertain young and old alike.

The North Yorkshire Moors Railway

The history of the Pickering to Whitby railway is fascinating. It was surveyed by George Stephenson and opened in 1836. For the first eleven years of its life the carriages were drawn by horses, not engines. On the downhill sections the horses were placed in dandy carts behind the carriages; the horses stood there while they and the carriages raced down the track at up to 30 m.p.h. The railway was connected to the larger network in 1845. It was taken over by George Hudson, the "Railway King", and modernised with steam locomotives on 1st July, 1847. The line finally closed under the Beeching Plan on March 6th, 1965.

Over the next few years the idea grew of turning one of the most scenic railways in England into a private line once more. By 1973 the North York Moors Historical Railway Trust had a membership of 7,000 and had raised £60,000 towards buying the line from British Rail. The line from Pickering to Grosmont was reopened by the Duchess of Kent on 1st May, 1973.

It is a splendid run through spectacular Newtondale, a steep-sided gorge covered in trees. The line continues over the moors to Goathland, an attractive moorland village with a number of waterfalls. The railway then descends to

Grosmont in the Esk valley. During the summer there is a connecting bus service to Whitby.

South of the Market Place

Birdgate leaves the top end of the Market Place and descends to the roundabout. The Black Swan Inn was the town's premier coaching inn and was used by the *Neptune* and *Royal Mail* stage coaches. The *Neptune* started running in 1832 from Leeds to Whitby, via York, Malton and Pickering, completing the journey in 10 hours and 15 minutes. By 1840 it had adapted to changing times – the journey over the moors to Whitby was undertaken on the railway.

When the Pickering – Whitby railway was opened on 26th May, 1836 the Black Swan wined and dined a party of 300 people, many of whom had come from Whitby on the inaugural run. The event is recorded on a plaque near the entrance which was unveiled by the Duchess of Kent when reopening the railway in 1973.

The road descends Smiddy Hill, a pleasant stretch of grass where art exhibitions are sometimes staged. Continue to the roundabout. The Forest and Vale Hotel was built about 1787 as a mansion called Low Hall.

The road to Scarborough passes along Eastgate. Near the junction is the large car park on the site of the former cattle market. The award winning Tourist Information Centre is in the two-storey building with an outside staircase. The friendly staff will help you with information and enough ideas to last a day or a week. The place also has an excellent variety of craft goods and books of local interest for sale.

Further along Eastgate is the Eastgate Square shopping centre of small shops. At the other side of the road is the bus station. Behind the houses at the north side of the road there used to be horse-racing stables and a besom factory. Besoms are traditional brushes made from heather; they were sold at markets and fairs and many were taken to the Tyneside shipyards where they were used to take the scum off molten metal.

Hungate goes westward from the roundabout towards

Helmsley. Looking into the rear entrance of the Black Swan Hotel you can easily imagine the mail coaches racing in and out of the yard and the ostlers rushing to change the horses.

Across the road is Houndgate Hall; it looks a plain uninteresting building but nothing could be further from the truth. On the wall is a plaque stating "Houndgate Hall. Dr. John Kirk B.A., M.B., B.C., founder of the Kirk Collection now in the Castle Museum, York, lived here from 1910 to 1938". Over those years he gathered together a fascinating collection of items of 19th century life. The doctor's round covered a large area visiting farms and villages on horseback. All the time he was looking for opportunities to buy the items that formed his collection. Some of the items were given to him to pay the bill – this was before the days of the National Health Service. The collection started off with police truncheons and firemarks and finished up with shop windows and a fire engine. Nearly every room in the house was filled including a man trap in the surgery!

The house was used as James Herriot's Skeldale House during the filming of the first full length film of *All Creatures Great and Small*. The room facing the roundabout was Dr. Kirk's surgery and during the filming was used as James Herriot's surgery. The dispensary where Dr. Kirk worked was used as the dispensary in the film.

A little further down the street is the old Methodist Chapel which is now the headquarters of the Pickering Musical Society. Rudyard Kipling's grandfather was minister here. His father was born in the minister's house, which used to stand in front of the chapel, on 6th July, 1837. At the back of the building is the old graveyard now grassed over. One gravestone remains to John Castillo. He was known as the Bard of the Dales and spent a great part of his life as a stonemason in the Esk Valley – some of his work can still be identified on bridges and buildings. He was also a Wesleyan preacher but he was especially noted for his dialect poems.

Bridge Street and the Museum

Heading west from the foot of the Market Place into Bridge Street you can see the railway station on the right. You may be lucky and see a steam engine in the station, with the engine partly hidden in smoke as the passengers alight.

At the other side of the road is the Beckside craft shop. The building dates back to 19th century when it was erected as a Methodist Chapel. It closed when the larger chapel opened in Potter Hill, and later became a soup kitchen, theatre and cinema. It has now been restored and put to a good use. The shop across the street still carries a firemark of the Yorkshire Insurance Company high on the wall.

As you cross the bridge there is a pleasant view upstream along Pickering Beck. To the left is the stone-built Regency building which is the Beck Isle Museum of Rural Life. It was originally built as an agricultural college by William Marshall, but he died in 1818 before it was completed. Both he and his brother were noted agriculturists; there is a plaque to William in the entrance. There are seventeen rooms filled with items of interest, each room having a different theme. There is a printer's shop and a cottage kitchen, a cobbler's shop and room displaying items on the local photographer Sidney Smith. Outside in the yard are a blacksmith's and wheelwright's shops and farm carts. The museum offers a fascinating glimpse of life in times past.

Castlegate, Pickering

BRIDGE STREET

SMIDDY HILL

PICKERING CASTLE.

17

THORNTON LE DALE

The Square

This is the area around the crossroads and market cross in the centre of the village. A footbridge near the old smithy gives easy access to the large car park in the grounds of the Hall. As you cross the first footbridge you can see that the stream flows in the opposite direction to the stream ten yards in front of you. Facing you across the road is the old Market Cross. John de Eston was granted a weekly market and two yearly fairs by Edward I on November 12th, 1281. The present tree-shaded green blends in well with the rest of the village. At the side of the cross is a pair of stocks. These are not the original stocks but a pair set up to replace them. They were made by William Wray & Son and built to accommodate two people. They were used for minor offences, the offenders usually being forced to sit in the stocks from dawn till dusk on market day.

Before the Second World War, Charlie Myers used to run the bus service with a 1922 Ford 14-seater. On Thursdays he would run into Scarborough and on Fridays and Saturdays to Malton. Occasionally the journey into Malton would be made via Yedingham if someone needed to be picked up. It was nothing unusual for a farmer to climb on board with a small pig or lamb under his arm! On Saturday nights he ran the "Picture Bus" to Pickering cinema. It was often said that passengers could have walked home quicker than Charlie drove.

The Smithy

Beyond the stream is The Forge gift shop which used to be the village smithy. Until the Second World War the smithy was operated by Ted and Charlie Roger. This was when it cost six shillings to make four horseshoes, fit them and dress the hooves – about two hours hard work. Les Roger recalled going down at six o' clock on a wet morning and seeing six horses waiting to be shod and another six waiting at the other smithy in Brook Lane. The smithy was more in demand by the farmers when the weather was bad. At the side of the entrance to the shop you can see the jig which was used to bend the iron tyres for wheels. There used to be a hooping plate for fixing the metal tyres to the wooden wheels near the stream. When the heated tyre had been fitted to the wheel the whole lot was thrown into the stream to contract it on to the rim. This was easier than pouring water on to the tyre as most blacksmiths had to do.

The New Inn was rebuilt in Georgian times. The manor court used to be held there. The Buck Inn at the other side of the crossroads dates from the seventeenth century and until late Victorian times had cruck beams. The Inn was the setting for a feast paid for by John Priestman. It was to thank the people who spent two hours fighting a fire in his tannery – though they only managed to save the brewhouse!

Chestnut Avenue

This street heads eastwards from the Square. On one side is Thornton Beck flowing beside the high wall enclosing the Hall's grounds. On the other side of the road are Lady Lumley's Almshouses, the gift of Elizabeth, Viscountess Lumley. They were built in 1670 to house four people from Thornton le Dale, six from Sinnington, one from Edstone and one from Ellerburn. Lady Lumley owned land in all these areas. In 1890 the occupants received £11-10s and a ton of coal per annum. At the end of the row of houses is the old Grammar School, also endowed by Lady Lumley. It was open to all children of Thornton le Dale and Sinnington who could read the English Testament. It had a spacious schoolroom capable of taking 200 pupils but in 1890 there were only sixteen scholars attending the school.

Continuing along the street you come to the bridge. The view upstream is without doubt one of the most picturesque in the North of England. The crystal-clear stream glides down under the bridge passing the thatched Beck Isle Cottage. It is a scene that has appeared on many calendars.

It is a delightful walk upstream from the bridge. The path passes Beck Isle Cottage and a number of seats and flower beds to reach Priestmans Lane. Here you can cross over the footbridge and turn left to the mill. Continue bearing left and the road leads round into Whitbygate and back to the crossroads.

The Mill

Milling has been carried on in Thornton le Dale since at least the 13th century. The present mill is set close to the beck. High on the side of the three-storey building is a plaque stating: "This mill was rebuilt and enlarged by G.F.G. Hill, A.D. 1919." Until the 1920s the mill derived some of its power from Thornton Beck. During the early 1920s Harry Burgess set up his own business making flour at Thornton Mill; this was where the popular Burgess Gold Medal plain and self raising flours were milled. In 1963 the mill adapted to the manufacturing of animal feeds. Since then the company has expanded.

Maltongate

This is the street which lies to the south of the Square. Flowing down the side is Thornton Beck with numerous small bridges across the water to allow people to reach their homes. The southern end of the street was the former village of Farmanby. Opposite the Post Office is the Hill Institute built in 1897 at a cost of £400 as a memorial to Squire J. R. Hill. In front of the Institute is a street plan of the village and the War Memorial to those who gave their lives in two World Wars. A little further down the street is Ellerburn Old Vicarage, built in 1890 for the Rev. A. J. Durrand. He used to ride out to his tiny church in a pony and trap. A new bridge over the stream allows access to the car park in the grounds of The Hall. Traditionally, John Wesley preached at Box Tree Farm in Maltongate probably on July 16th, 1766 when he was travelling from Scarborough to Middleton.

At the end of Maltongate is the old railway station, now a caravan park. The Scarborough to Pickering railway line was opened on May 1st, 1882 and the arrival of the first train was a day of celebration. It was met by an assembly of people at each station on the line. Bunting was hung out and anyone buying a ticket that day could make as many journeys as they liked. Between the two World Wars the fare to Scarborough was 2s 6d single or 4s 6d return and a Saturday excursion trip used to cost one shilling return. Sentinel railcars used to run on the line in the summer months carrying as many as 300 passengers each trip. The line closed on June 1st, 1950.

The route back to The Square can be varied by turning left after a hundred yards along Roxby Road. As you approach the Pickering road, you pass a children's playground with swings, shute and a climbing frame. At the end of Roxby Road turn right back to the Square.

The Hall

On the right of the road leading to the church are the grounds and buildings of the Hall, formerly the home of the Hill family who were local landowners. At the turn of this century there used to be chained foxes outside the entrance. Traditionally, Richard Johnson Hill staked the manor of Thornton on a game of billiards with George Osbaldestone – fortunately the game was stopped by Lord Middleton. It is now a residential home for retired people but there is still a bar and riding stables open to the public.

The Church of All Saints

The church stands on some raised ground just beyond the Hall. The present structure dates from the 14th century but the Norman font is from an earlier church. Sir Richard Chomley, the Black Knight of the North, was buried in the chancel in May 1583. There is a fine wall tomb surmounted by the figure of a lady, probably the tomb of Lady Beatrice Hastings who lived in the reign of Edward II. The oldest brass in the church is in memory of John Porter, a London merchant who died in 1686.

In the churchyard are two interesting gravestones. One tells its own story: "In memory of Matthew Grimes who died October 30th, 1875, aged 96 years. An old soldier who served in the 20th and 24th Infantry in India and the Peninsular Wars. Guard at St. Helena over Napoleon and a bearer of that monarch to his grave. This monument is erected by admiring friends of an old veteran." The grave is about 20 yards from the church on the east side. The other interesting stone is over the grave of James Booth. It states: "Well done, good and faithful servant." For 56 years he was gamekeeper and huntsman to Richard Hill who erected the stone.

Brook Lane

This small street turns off Whitbygate near the toilets. The lane passes a number of stone-built houses with colourful gardens. At the end is a former smithy now used by Brook Motors as a garage. On the left of the junction is a small fenced-off green; this is the pinfold where stray animals were impounded by the pinder. They could be reclaimed on payment of a small fine. The lane to the left leads up to the road to Ellerburn. On the left is the Old House which was leased to the Overseer of the Poor in 1734. The building contained an underground cell known as the "Black Hole" which was used as a village prison as late as 1850. The last prisoner was a woman and four men forced their way into the cell and released her.

Cottage in Maltongate, Thornton le Dale

Cottages at Ellerburn

ELLERBURN

This peaceful little hamlet lies a mile up Thornton Dale. It can be reached by car from Whitbygate, the road turning right then left on the outskirts of the village. Or you can walk across the fields as detailed in Walk 3. The road to the hamlet passes along the foot of a wooded hillside with the church set in the valley below.

Parts of the church of St. Hilda date from before the Norman Conquest, but most of the building is thirteenth century. The entrance is through a stone lych gate with a wooden roof. If you look carefully at the stonework of the church porch you can see that part of a stone cross has been built into the porch. On the left of the window in the south wall is part of a churchyard cross inscribed with gagged serpents.

The inside of the church is lit by three brass paraffin lamps and there are also two bracket candle holders. The font, possibly pre-Conquest, is a plain bowl with no decoration; it stands on four pillars with a central stem.

The peaceful valley once had a number of industries including two paper mills. About 1817 the Low Mill produced four tons of paper per annum, mainly from linen rags. The farm opposite the entrance to the church used to be a bleach mill, and as late as 1830 forty webs could be seen stretched out in the fields to dry. John Raw was the last clogmaker to work up the valley. Up to the First World War he cut clog soles from alder logs; these were carted down to Thornton le Dale and placed in large honeycomb piles to dry. They were later transferred to Lancashire for the mill hands to wear.

DALBY FOREST DRIVE

Low Dalby is a picturesque village in the North Riding Forest Park. It is 3½ miles by road from Thornton le Dale or it can be reached by Walk 4. It lies on a Forestry Commission toll road which winds its way through the forest and into the Derwent Valley. A return to Thornton le Dale can be made up Troutsdale to Snainton or along Forge Valley to West Ayton. There are a number of Nature Trails waymarked from the Forest Drive. There is an information centre in Low Dalby with an interpretive display on the Forestry Commission's work. Further along the trail is the Bridestones car park near Staindale Lake. A walk from the car park leads to a number of sandstone outcrops on Grime Moor that have been carved by the weather into unusual shapes. Some of the huge stones stand on narrow bases.

The Bridestones

SOME WALKS IN THE AREA

Walk 1. Pickering to Thornton le Dale.
(2½ miles, 5 miles return).

From the roundabout in Pickering take the Whitby road and turn right after 100 yards along Ruffa Lane, carrying straight on when the tarmac road ends. After a quarter of a mile cross a stile beside a gate and continue with the hedge on your right. At the end of the field turn left to a stile. At the junction turn right through the wood to a gate into a field; keep the fence on your right to a gate below the farm. Turn left along the farm track over a cattle grid, then in 20 yards turn right through a gate into a wood. The path rises through the wood to reach a field corner; continue with the hedge on your left to a stile. Cross over the fields and after four stiles the path bears right to a stile onto the road. Turn left down into Thornton le Dale.

Walk 2. A stroll past Roxby Manor (1 mile).

From the crossroads in Thornton le Dale walk along the road towards Scarborough and turn left down Brook Lane. Fork right past Brook Motors and continue on the path to the road. Turn left to the junction and take the path marked public footpath opposite. Walk up the path and along the edge of the wood to a gate into a field. On the left is a pleasant view over the rooftops of Thornton le Dale. Turn left in the field and descend to a gate, cross over the access road and pass through the gate opposite. Keep the hedge on your right to the end of the field where you turn right down some steps and continue to the main road where you can turn left to the crossroads.

Walk 3. Ellerburn.

From The Square, Thornton le Dale, walk along Chestnut Avenue to the bridge. Turn left on the riverside path past the thatched cottage and cross the footbridge into Priestmans Lane. Turn left towards the mill and fork right at the public footpath sign down the side of the mill. A stile leads back to the riverside. Eventually you turn right at the end of a field to a stile on your left and continue over the fields. Pass to the left of the farm and cross the bridge to reach the church. You can return by the same route or along the road. On the outskirts of Thornton le Dale turn right, then left, down Whitbygate to the crossroads.

Walk 4. Low Dalby. (7½ miles).

Follow the same route as Walk 3 to Ellerburn. Pass through the hamlet and continue along the quiet road. Turn right across the bridge about ¼-mile beyond the church. The road bears left passing Low and High Paper Mill farms and eventually becomes a hardcore forestry road passing beneath the trees in Dalby Forest. Keep Dalby Beck on your left until you reach Low Dalby where there is an interpretive centre on the Forestry Commission's work. You can return by the same route or follow the Forest Drive road which climbs back out of the valley. At the road junction turn left back to Thornton le Dale.

Walk 5. Country Lanes (2¼ miles).

From The Square, Thornton le Dale, walk along Chestnut Avenue and cross the bridge. Take the first turn right beyond the Hall along Dog Kennel Lane. Bear right at the South Lane junction up the hill and turn right at the T-junction along a pleasant rural lane. It may be worth looking for wild flowers in the hedgerows. Take the first turn right along another lane. At the end turn right to reach two footbridges which cross the streams to reach Maltongate. Turn right up the street back to the crossroads.

PLACES TO VISIT

For more details of the area to the north of Pickering see *Exploring the North York Moors*. For the area to the south of Pickering see *Exploring York's Countryside*. Both are published by Dalesman Books.

Flamingo Land

Four miles south of Pickering at Kirby Misperton is the Flamingo Land Zoo and Funpark. There are dolphin shows and a jungle zoo, a cable car, monorail, spectacular rides and an indoor Funhouse and Play centre. This makes a day out for all the family.

Great Edstone

An interesting hill top village standing above the low lying valley of the river Rye. Over the entrance to the church is a Saxon sundial. A translation of the Latin inscription reads: "The wayfarer's clock: Lothan made me." The dial has the day divided into eight "hours". There is a fine view over the surrounding valley from the churchyard.

The next four villages can be visited in one circular drive from Pickering.

Newton on Rawcliffe

The road to the village leaves Pickering past the railway station. The stone-built houses stand around the long green which has a pond. Close by is the Mel House Bird and Animal Garden. It has an interesting collection of birds and animals ranging from farm animals to Vietnamese pigs and wallabies to terrapins. Children can feed the animals while parents visit the cafe or craft shop. On the northern side of the village a track leads to a seat with a spectacular view over Newtondale. Two miles north is the start of the Newtondale nature trail and the Newtondale Forest Drive (toll road) to Levisham.

PLACES to VISIT near THORNTON-LE-DALE

Lilla Cross

Kirkbymoorside

The Crypt ~ Lastingham church

Lastingham

This delightful village lies on the edge of the moors; there is a fine view from the cross on the Appleton le Moors road. The stone houses cluster around Hole Beck and one of the village wells stand beside the bridge. The interesting church has a crypt nearly 1,000 years old which is reached by a flight of steps inside the church.

Hutton le Hole

This is one of the most picturesque villages in the North of England; it nestles in a hollow on the edge of the moors. Hutton Beck flows through the centre and the green is kept short by the sheep. In the centre of the village is the Ryedale Folk Museum which shows many aspects of life on the moors. There are many reconstructed buildings and craft workshops at the rear of the museum. Two miles away is Farndale well-known for its display of wild daffodils in April.

Sinnington

This attractive village is just off the Pickering to Kirkbymoorside road. The stone-built houses stand around the large green which is crossed by the river Seven. The interesting church stands above the village.

Malton

Standing in the attractive Market Place is Malton Museum. It has displays on the Romans from the nearby fort and other displays on local history which change regularly. Just off the Pickering Road is Eden Camp and Eden Farm Insight. The camp was built for prisoners of war and the huts now house displays on many aspects of World War II. Eden Farm Insight is a working farm with a museum, blacksmith's forge, farm walks and of course animals.

Goathland and Grosmont can be reached by car or the North Yorkshire Moors Railway.

Goathland

This widely scattered village is surrounded by moors and wooded valleys. The area offers some delightful walks to Darnholme, Beck Hole or to the Roman road over the moors. There are nine waterfalls in the area; the highest is Mallyan Spout reached by a path down the side of the Mallyan Hotel.

Grosmont

The village is set on a steep hillside overlooking the Murk Esk with the railway station at the foot of the hill. A 3½ mile Historic Railway Trail connects Grosmont and Goathland. The return journey can be made on the train. It follows the original railway line of 1836.

Newton upon Rawcliffe